CARTOON·NATION presents

EST. 1776

THE U.S. SUPREME COURT

by Danny Fingeroth
illustrated by Cynthia Martin

CONSULTANT:
Michael Bailey
Colonel William J. Walsh Associate Professor
of American Government
Georgetown University, Washington, D.C.

Capstone press

Mankato, Minnesota

Graphic Library is published by Capstone Press,
151 Good Counsel Drive, P.O. Box 669, Mankato, Minnesota 56002.
www.capstonepress.com

1 2 3 4 5 6 13 12 11 10 09 08

Library of Congress Cataloging-in-Publication Data
Fingeroth, Danny.
    The U.S. Supreme Court / by Danny Fingeroth; illustrated by Cynthia Martin.
    p. cm. — (Graphic library. Cartoon nation)
    Includes bibliographical references and index.
    Summary: "In cartoon format, explains the history, role, and responsibilities of the U.S.
Supreme Court in United States government" — Provided by publisher.
    ISBN-13: 978-1-4296-1985-1 (hardcover)
    ISBN-10: 1-4296-1985-6 (hardcover)
    ISBN-13: 978-1-4296-2857-0 (softcover pbk.)
    ISBN-10: 1-4296-2857-X (softcover pbk.)
    1. United States. Supreme Court — History — Juvenile literature. 2. Judicial power —
United States — History — Juvenile literature. 3. United States. Supreme Court — History.
I. Martin, Cynthia, 1961– II. Title. III. Title: United States Supreme Court. IV. Series.
KF8742.F56 2009
347.73'12 — dc22   2008000486

Art Director and Designer
Bob Lentz

Production Designer
Kim Brown

Colorist
Krista Ward

Cover Artist
Kelly Brown

Editor
Christopher L. Harbo

EST. CARTOON·NATION 1776

TABLE OF CONTENTS

Arguments are part of life. Even good friends can disagree. And competition almost always leads to disagreements. For instance, baseball players often argue over whether a fly ball is fair or foul.

Fair by far!

Foul by a mile!

Sometimes it takes a third person to help settle a disagreement. In baseball, umpires decide who's right.

The United States' court system plays a similar role to that of baseball umpires. Of course, a court case is much more serious than a baseball game. Courts settle issues or problems between people or businesses.

verdict — the decision on an issue in a court case

There are several types of courts. These can generally be divided into local, state, and federal.

Local courts take care of everyday matters, such as parking tickets.

State courts rule on more serious matters, such as robbery or murder.

Federal courts rule on cases that deal with United States government law.

If people are unhappy with a court decision, they can ask a state or federal court to hear their case.

When people are still not satisfied with a verdict, they can ask the Supreme Court to review the case. The Supreme Court is like the "head umpire." The Supreme Court's ruling is final.

What's the ninth guy going to do?

I don't know, but one of us isn't going to like it.

TYPES OF CASES

Like all courts, the Supreme Court hears both civil and criminal cases. In a civil case, there is a disagreement between people. In a criminal case, a person is accused of a crime. Criminal cases are brought by governments, not by individuals.

The Constitution was also vague about the powers of the Court. In 1803, the case of *Marbury versus Madison* helped establish just what those powers were.

> . . . and you're hired . . . and you're hired . . . and you're hired . . .

> Yahoo! Dental coverage. No more wooden teeth!

WILLIAM MARBURY

JOHN ADAMS

In 1800, President John Adams lost his bid for reelection to Thomas Jefferson. Before leaving office, Adams appointed many of his friends to government jobs, including William Marbury.

Annoyed that so many of Adams' pals had been given jobs, Jefferson ignored Marbury's appointment. He ordered his secretary of state, future president James Madison, not to give Marbury the promised job.

> We'll show that Adams, won't we, James?

JAMES MADISON

> You said it, boss.

THOMAS JEFFERSON

Marbury went to court to get his job back. Congress said the Supreme Court had the right to hear such cases. But Chief Justice John Marshall was afraid that if the Court ruled for Marbury, Jefferson would ignore the decision. He didn't want the Court to appear weak.

So Marshall ruled that the Constitution had never given Congress the right to make such a law about the Court. Therefore, he said the Court shouldn't hear Marbury's case. Marbury lost because the last court that had heard the case had ruled against him.

JOHN MARSHALL

I hope that's clear to everybody.

WILLIAM MARBURY

I guess wooden teeth aren't so bad after all.

With his ruling, Marshall established the principle of "judicial review." *Marbury versus Madison* made the Supreme Court more powerful. The Court could now overturn laws that went against the Constitution.

Well, is this law okay?

Don't rush me.

PRESIDENTIAL APPOINTMENTS

The president can appoint a chief justice to lead the Court when the position is open. Presidents can promote a current justice. Or they can name a new justice to lead the court. The Senate must approve the president's choice.

If you lose a decision in a lower court, you can appeal your case to the Supreme Court. Cases for appeal come from state or lower federal courts. An appeal occurs if the loser in a lower court feels he or she lost unfairly. Cases may be brought by a person, company, city, or state.

But just bringing an appeal doesn't guarantee your case will be heard by the Supreme Court. About 7,000 cases a year are submitted to the Supreme Court. The Court agrees to hear about 100 of them. The Court hears cases it believes involve key issues about the meaning of the Constitution.

A case can take months or years to make its way to the Supreme Court. Once it is accepted for review, the Court makes a relatively speedy decision. Once the lawyers have their say, the justices often return a ruling the same week.

The Supreme Court is in session from October until late June or early July. But even during their summer break, the justices review requests for cases to be heard in the next term. And in rare instances, a case may be so urgent that they will hear it during the summer.

appeal — to ask another court to review a case already decided by a lower court

The Supreme Court has two main jobs. The Court's first job is deciding if a lower court has ruled correctly. The Court may feel that part of the Constitution applies to the case. In that event, they may decide to hear the case's appeal.

This is one dense document.

And what it doesn't say is as important as what it does say.

The Supreme Court's second job is to decide whether a law is constitutional. But the Court does not decide on its own to review a law. The justices only rule on a law if a case regarding that law is brought before them.

Sometimes justices feel that any constitutional issue in a case has already been addressed. In that event, they can refuse to hear the case. Cases that are refused by the Supreme Court are sent back to the lower courts.

No, no, no! Back to the lower courts you go!

The Court may also decide to hear a case if it has great national importance. In 1971, the Court ruled that *The New York Times* could print secret documents it received from a former government employee. This ruling established that in certain situations, freedom of the press was more important than government secrecy.

And Supreme Court justices take their duties very seriously. For instance, Justice Louis Brandeis was known for rewriting rulings many times until he got them just right.

Becoming a Justice

There are no rules about who can and cannot become a Supreme Court justice.

Candidates for the job have always been lawyers or judges. However, a law degree or law background is not required.

The president nominates people to be on the Court. Usually, these people share the president's views on matters relating to law and the Constitution. But each justice is still an individual with his or her own opinions. Sometimes a justice will vote differently on a case than the president thought they would.

nominate — to suggest that someone would be the right person to do a job

Nominees for the Supreme Court are approved or rejected by the Senate. The approval process can be heated. After all, justices have a lot of influence on how laws and the Constitution are interpreted. And once approved, justices serve for the rest of their lives or until they decide to retire.

TOUGH APPROVALS

Most Court nominees are eventually approved by the Senate. But a nominee's personal and work histories are looked at very closely. The process can be unpleasant, but the Senate wants to put the most qualified people on the bench.

In recent decades, Robert Bork and Clarence Thomas had notably nasty approval hearings. Bork was rejected. Thomas was accepted and still serves on the Court today.

Before the justices sit down to discuss a case, they shake hands with one another. Shaking hands is a Court tradition. It reminds justices that they are committed to being respectful of one another, even if they disagree.

Getting all nine justices to agree is downright difficult. But that's not necessary for a Court decision. Majority rules.

Only five justices need to agree to make the Court's decision final. A Supreme Court decision is called an opinion.

If the chief justice is among the majority, he writes the opinion. He can also assign another justice to write it. Sometimes the chief justice doesn't agree with the majority. In those cases, the justice in the majority who has been on the Court the longest writes the opinion.

After an opinion is announced, it gets published in a Supreme Court record. This information is often reported in newspapers.

majority — more than half of a group of people

CHANGING THE CONSTITUTION

As the American public's ideas and attitudes change, so do the laws passed by Congress. Likewise, the Supreme Court can change its mind. When it does, this is called "reversing a decision."

> Sometimes going backward is the best way to make progress.

> Ah! I feel like a new document!

This ability of the Court to change its mind reflects the brilliance of the Constitution. It can be changed to meet the needs of the nation.

If citizens believe a change is needed, the Constitution can even be changed or amended. Amending the Constitution is not easy. Once a change in the Constitution is passed, the Supreme Court must take that amendment into account when making new decisions.

> You'll have to try harder than that if you're going to change me!

Adding an amendment to the Constitution is a rare event. Between 1788 and 2008, only 27 amendments have been made to the Constitution.

$$220 \div 27 = 8.14815$$

Constitution ratified in 1788

Can't we use a calculator?

That's an average of one amendment about every eight years. With so few changes, it's obvious the Founding Fathers got the Constitution right the first time.

IMPORTANT AMENDMENTS

The first 10 amendments to the Constitution, known as the Bill of Rights, were approved in 1791. These amendments gave people important rights like freedom of speech, freedom of religion, and freedom of the press. Here are a few other important amendments that have changed the Constitution over the years:

The 13th Amendment ended slavery in 1865.

The 15th Amendment gave African American men the right to vote in 1870.

The 19th Amendment gave women the right to vote in 1920.

The Supreme Court's rulings often affect people's day-to-day lives. Sometimes these changes are considered positive by most people. Other times, they are considered negative.

For example, an 1896 case actually made racial discrimination and segregation legal. Here's how it happened. After the Union won the Civil War in 1865, African American slaves were freed. But in many states, white leaders passed laws that kept African Americans from important rights, including voting.

In 1892, an African American man named Homer Plessy was arrested for sitting in a "whites only" train. Plessy argued in a Louisiana court that the law was unconstitutional. Judge John H. Ferguson was the presiding judge.

How can it be illegal for me to sit peacefully on a train? That's not fair.

Who ever said life was fair?

Ferguson ruled against him. So Plessy sued Ferguson, and the case ended up at the Supreme Court in 1896. But the Supreme Court ruled against Plessy. It decided that "separate but equal" treatment of African Americans was acceptable. *Plessy versus Ferguson* allowed racial discrimination and segregation to continue.

By 1951, views about the relationship between African Americans and whites were changing. Oliver Brown and many other African Americans sued the school district of Topeka, Kansas. The district would not allow Brown's daughter to attend a school in her own neighborhood because it taught only white students.

In 1954, *Brown versus Board of Education of Topeka* reached the Supreme Court. The Court decided that "separate but equal" was not good enough. Often, African Americans were not treated equally. The Court's decision reversed *Plessy* and made segregation illegal.

Supreme Court rulings affect you more than you may realize. A ruling about e-mail privacy may not seem like it affects you. But you might feel differently about it if the FBI wanted to read your e-mail.

I just want a little peek at what he's writing.

Sorry. No can do.

Here are some specific examples of the Court's major impact on our lives:

MIRANDA VERSUS ARIZONA

If you've ever seen a police drama on TV, you've heard an arresting officer tell the person being arrested his rights. The officer says "you have the right to remain silent . . . ." These rights are known as Miranda Rights.

I'm going to read you your Miranda Rights.

You've got the wrong guy. My name isn't Miranda.

Miranda Rights come from the 1966 *Miranda versus Arizona* Supreme Court decision. That case established that a suspect must be told his or her rights to remain silent and to get a lawyer when arrested.

BUSH VERSUS GORE

In presidential elections, each state has a certain number of electoral votes. The candidate with the most popular votes in each state gets all of that state's electoral votes. The candidate who gets the most electoral votes wins the election.

You can stop counting.

Thank goodness. These punch card ballots were making my eyes buggy.

In the 2000 election, Al Gore won the popular vote. But George W. Bush won the electoral votes by a very small amount. Gore demanded a recount to be sure the results were correct. But the Supreme Court ruled in Bush's favor and said the recounts had to stop. Because he had more electoral votes, Bush became president.

TURN OVER THE TAPES

President Richard Nixon tape-recorded his White House meetings. In 1974, a judge demanded Nixon's tapes as part of the investigation into the Watergate scandal. Nixon refused to turn over the tapes, saying they contained presidential secrets.

Speak into the plant, please.

The Supreme Court disagreed. The Court ordered Nixon to turn over the tapes. The tapes revealed that Nixon had lied about knowing that crimes had been committed. He resigned the presidency later that year.

FAMOUS JUSTICES

They may not be movie or sports stars, but there have been some famous Supreme Court justices.

Chief Justice John Marshall served from 1801 to 1835. Through clever constitutional interpretation, he made the Court equal to the other branches of government.

Chief Justice Earl Warren served from 1953 to 1969. He often disagreed with the man who appointed him, President Dwight D. Eisenhower. Warren would go on to head the group that investigated President John F. Kennedy's 1963 assassination.

EARL WARREN

This should be the last word on the topic.

That's what you think!

Other important justices include Thurgood Marshall and Sandra Day O'Connor. Marshall served from 1967 to 1991. He was the first African American justice. He had been a lawyer for the Brown family in *Brown versus Board of Education of Topeka*.

We were firsts —

THURGOOD MARSHALL

SANDRA DAY O'CONNOR

— but not lasts.

O'Connor served from 1981 to 2006. She was the first female justice. Before joining the Court, she had been assistant attorney general and a state senator in Arizona.

Each person who brings a case before the Court has his or her own reason for doing so. But the Court's role, by its nature, rises above the desires of any specific person.

The Court often rides the waves of social currents when choosing cases. Sometimes these are extremely **controversial** cases. In all cases, the Court must weigh individual rights against the needs of the majority of people.

Often, the Court must make its decisions in the midst of highly emotional situations. People who bring a case to the Supreme Court have exhausted every other legal option.

The members of the Court cannot let any personal tragedies they see or hear about sway them. Their job is to interpret the Constitution as calmly and logically as possible. Their decisions affect more than any one person.

What the justices decide can affect everyone in the country. Their decisions affect your local police, your teachers, your parents — and even you!

controversial — something that causes a lot of argument

TIME LINE

1788 — The U.S. Constitution is ratified. It states that "the judicial power of the United States shall be vested in one Supreme Court."

February 1, 1790 — The Supreme Court meets for the first time in New York City.

FEBRUARY 1, 1790

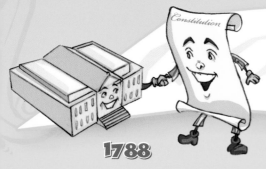

1788

May 17, 1954 — In the *Brown versus Board of Education of Topeka* decision, the Court establishes that "separate but equal" treatment of African Americans is not acceptable.

June 13, 1966 — The *Miranda versus Arizona* decision says that criminal suspects must be informed of their rights.

MAY 17, 1954

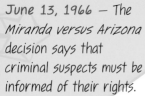

JUNE 13, 1966

October 2, 1967 — Thurgood Marshall becomes the first African American to join the Court.

OCTOBER 2, 1967

February 4, 1801 — John Marshall begins his term as chief justice.

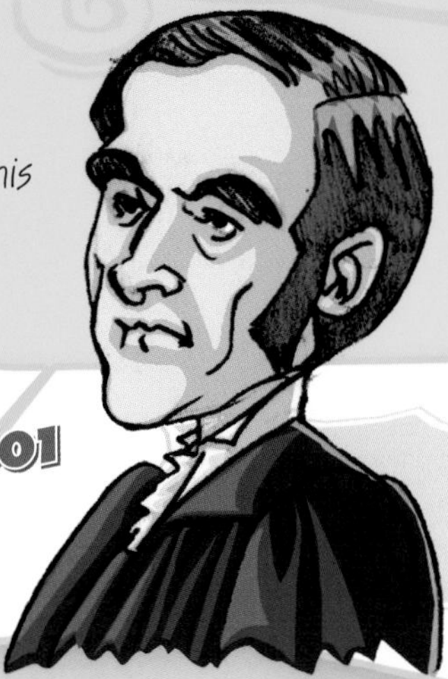

FEBRUARY 4, 1801

February 24, 1803 — In *Marbury versus Madison*, John Marshall declares the Supreme Court can overrule a law of Congress. This ruling establishes "judicial review."

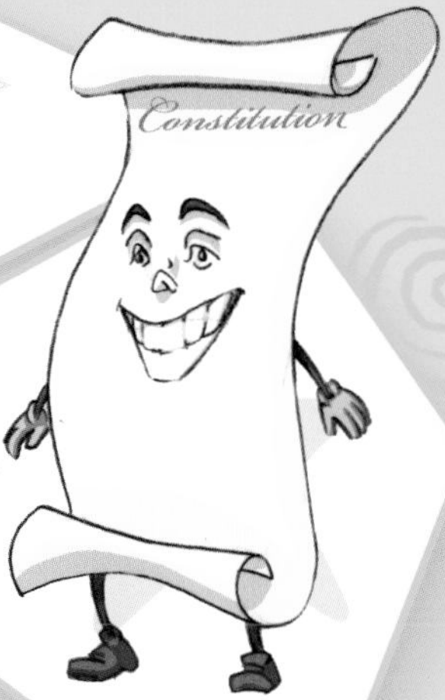
Constitution

FEBRUARY 24, 1803

May 18, 1896 — The Court's ruling in *Plessy versus Ferguson* says that African Americans and whites may have separate but equal facilities.

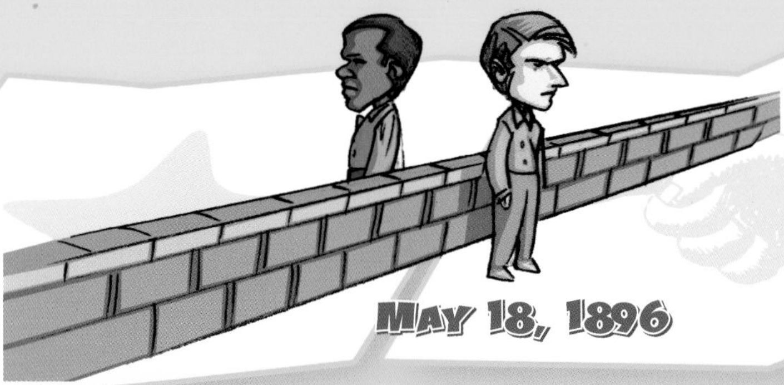

MAY 18, 1896

September 25, 1981 — Sandra Day O'Connor becomes the first woman to join the Supreme Court.

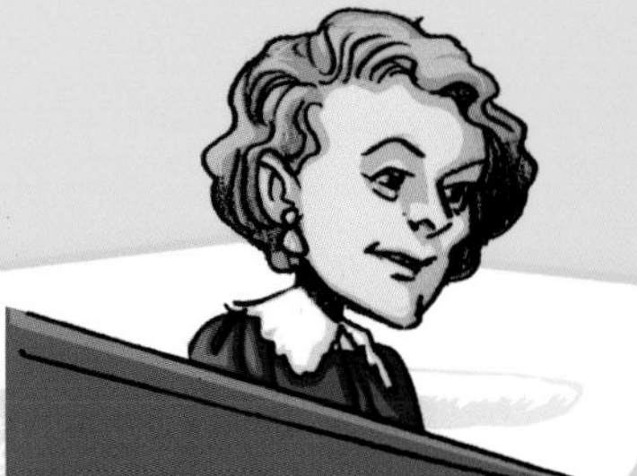

SEPTEMBER 25, 1981

December 12, 2000 — The *Bush versus Gore* decision stops recounts in the presidential election, giving the presidency to George W. Bush.

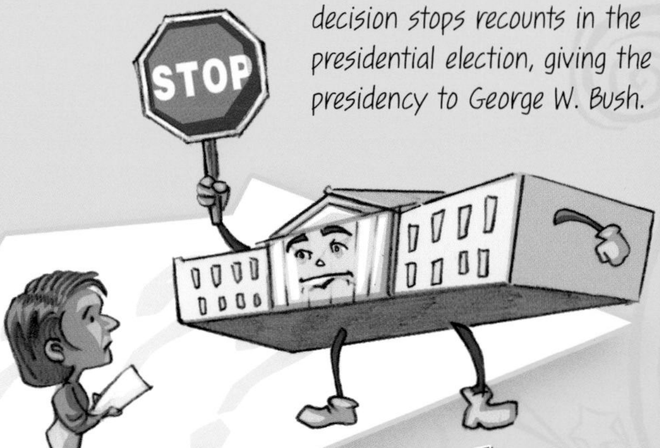
STOP

DECEMBER 12, 2000

GLOSSARY

amendment (uh-MEND-muhnt) — a change made to a law or a legal document

appeal (uh-PEEL) — to ask another court to review a case already decided by a lower court

Bill of Rights (BIL UHV RITES) — a list of 10 amendments to the Constitution that protect your right to speak freely, to practice religion, and other important rights

citizen (SI-tuh-zuhn) — a member of a country or state who has the right to live there

constitution (kon-stuh-TOO-shuhn) — the system of laws that state the rights of the people and the powers of the government

discrimination (dis-kri-muh-NAY-shuhn) — unfair treatment of others based on age, race, gender, or other differences

Founding Father (FOUN-ding FAH-thur) — one of a handful of men who were important in helping the colonies become one country

interpret (in-TUR-prit) — to decide what something means

majority (muh-JOR-uh-tee) — more than half of a group of people

nominate (NOM-uh-nate) — to suggest that someone would be the right person to do a job

segregation (seg-ruh-GAY-shuhn) — separating people because of their skin color

verdict (VUR-dikt) — the decision on an issue in a court case

veto (VEE-toh) — the power or right to stop a bill from becoming law

READ MORE

Beier, Anne. *The Supreme Court and the Judicial Branch*. A Primary Source Library of American Citizenship. New York: Rosen, 2004.

Dubois, Muriel L. *The U.S. Supreme Court*. Our Government. Mankato, Minn.: Capstone Press, 2004.

Sergis, Diana K. *Bush v. Gore: Controversial Presidential Election Case*. Landmark Supreme Court Cases. Berkeley Heights, N.J.: Enslow, 2003.

Taylor-Butler, Christine. *Thurgood Marshall*. Rookie Biographies. New York: Children's Press, 2006.

Wagner, Heather Lehr. *The Supreme Court*. The U.S. Government: How It Works. New York: Chelsea House, 2007.

INTERNET SITES

FactHound offers a safe, fun way to find Internet sites related to this book. All of the sites on FactHound have been researched by our staff.

Here's how:
1. Visit www.facthound.com
2. Choose your grade level.
3. Type in this book ID 1429619856 for age-appropriate sites. You may also browse subjects by clicking on letters, or by clicking on pictures and words.
4. Click on the Fetch It button.

FactHound will fetch the best sites for you!

INDEX